Just Voices
Gospel

NOVELLO PUBLISHING LIMITED
part of The Music Sales Group
London / New York / Paris / Sydney / Copenhagen / Berlin / Madrid / Tokyo

Amazing Grace

Words & Music by John Newton

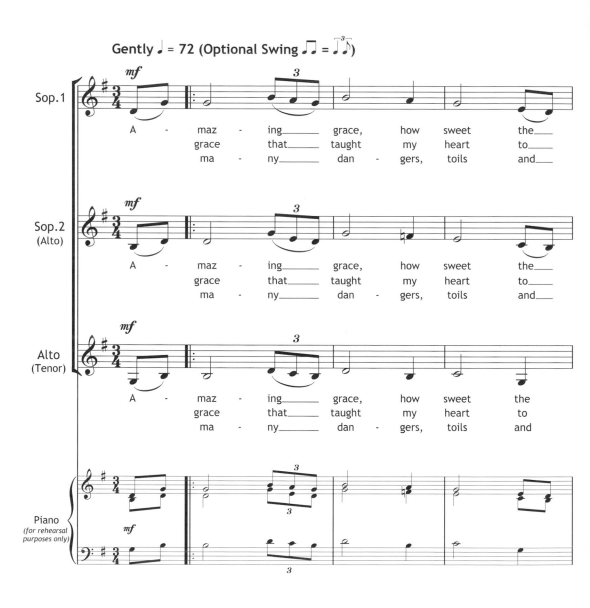

3

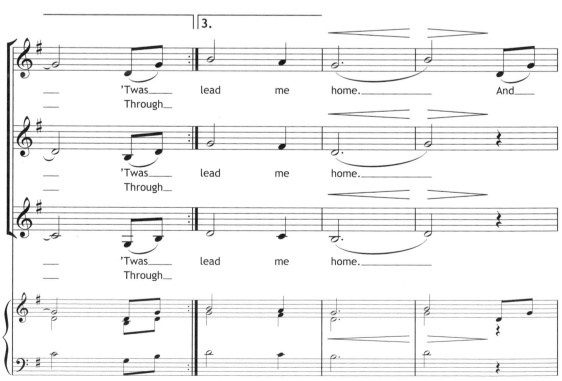

grace will___ lead me home._____ And___

Grace will lead me home.

Grace will lead me home._____

rit.

grace will lead_____ me__ home._____

Grace will lead me home._____

Grace will lead me home._____

Down By The Riverside

Traditional Spiritual

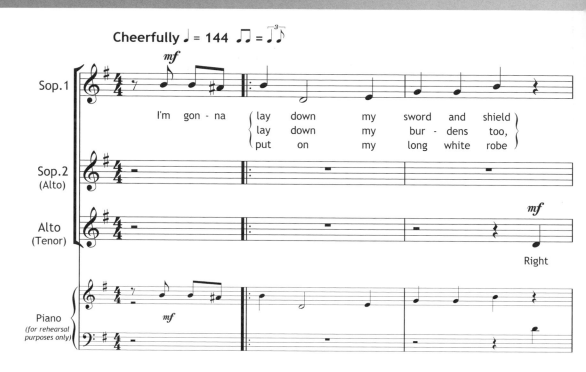

riv - er - side,___ down by___ the riv - er - side,___ I'm gon-na

riv - er - side,___ right there, down by___ the riv - er - side,___

riv - er - side,___ down by___ the riv - er - side,___

lay   down   my   sword   and   shield
lay   down   my   bur - dens   too,
put   on   my   long   white   robe

down   by_____   the

down   by_____   the

Right   there,   down   by_____   the

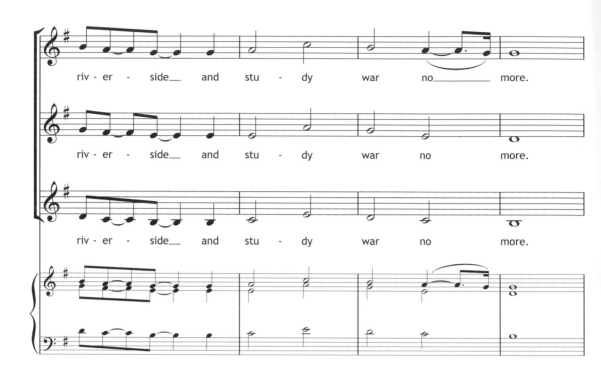

riv - er - side___ and stu - dy war no_____ more.

riv - er - side___ and stu - dy war no more.

riv - er - side___ and stu - dy war no more.

I ain't go - na stu - dy war___ no more,

I ain't go - na stu - dy war___ no more,

I ain't go - na stu - dy war___ no more, ain't gon - na

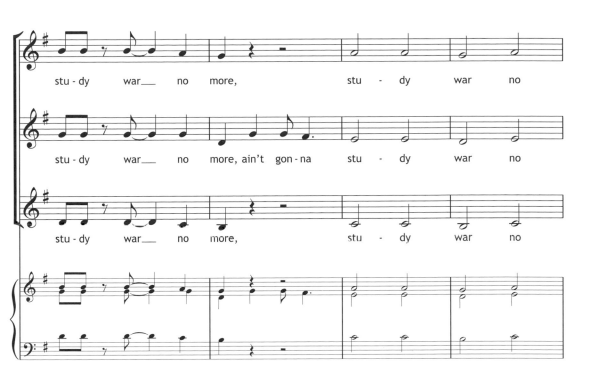

9

stu - dy war__ no more, I ain't gon-na stu - dy war no__

stu - dy war__ no more, stu - dy war no

stu - dy war__ no more, stu - dy war no

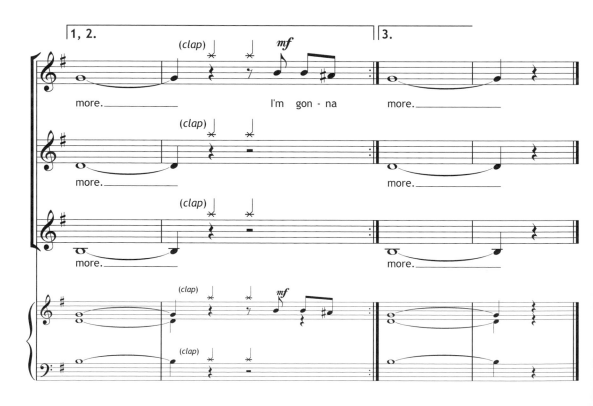

1, 2.   **3.**

more._____ I'm gon - na more._____

more._____ more._____

more._____ more._____

Lean On Me

WORDS & MUSIC BY BILL WITHERS

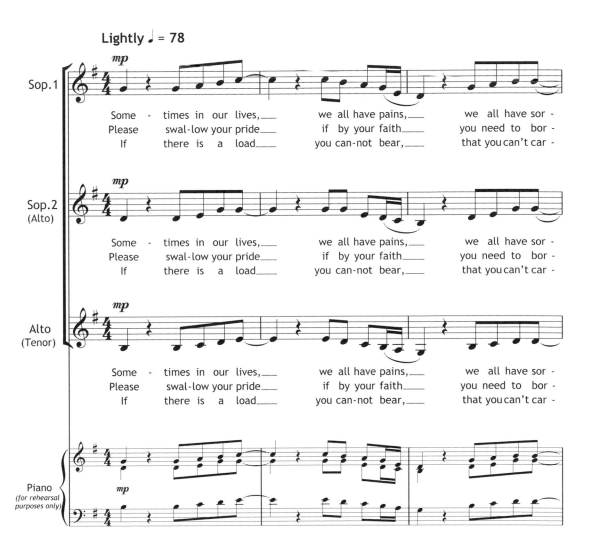

- rows.___ But if we are wise,___ yes, we know that there's___
- row.___ I'm right up the road___ and I'll share your load___
- ry, I'm right up the road,___ yes, I'll share your load,___

- rows.___ But if we are wise,___ yes, we know that there's___
- row.___ I'm right up the road___ and I'll share your load___
- ry, I'm right up the road,___ yes, I'll share your load,___

- rows.___ But if we are wise,___ yes, we know that there's___
- row.___ I'm right up the road___ and I'll share your load___
- ry,___ I'm right up the road,___ yes, I'll share your load,___

1. **2, 3.** *mf*

___ al-ways to - mor - row.___ call___ me. Lean on me,___ when you're not strong,___
___ if you just
___ if you just

___ al-ways to - mor - row.___ call me. Lean on me,___ when___ you're not strong,___
___ if you just
___ if you just

___ al-ways to - mor - row.___ call me. Lean on me,___ when you're not strong,___
___ if you just
___ if you just

I'll be your friend,___ I'll help you car - ry__ on.__ For it won't be long__

I'll be your friend,___ I'll help you car - ry__ on.__ For it won't be long__

I'll be your friend,___ I'll help you car - ry on.__ For it won't be long__

D.C. al Coda
Fine

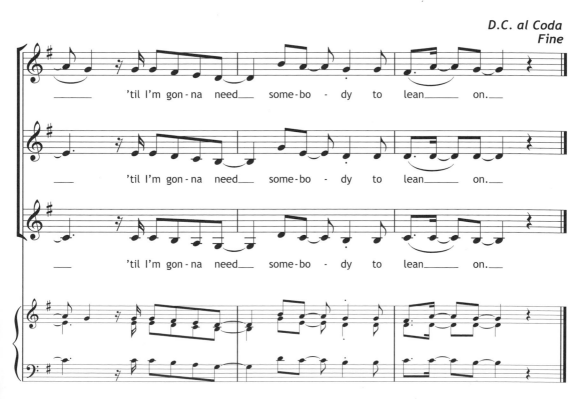

___ 'til I'm gon - na need__ some-bo - dy to lean____ on.__

___ 'til I'm gon - na need__ some-bo - dy to lean____ on.__

___ 'til I'm gon - na need__ some-bo - dy to lean____ on.__

13

Let It Be

Words & Music by John Lennon & Paul McCartney

find my-self in times of trou-ble Moth-er Ma-ry comes to me,
when the bro-ken heart-ed peo-ple liv-ing in the world a-gree,
when then night is cloud-y there is still a light that shines on me,

find my-self in times of trou-ble Moth-er Ma-ry comes to me,
when the bro-ken heart-ed peo-ple liv-ing in the world a-gree,
when then night is cloud-y there is still a light that shines on me,

find my-self in times of trou-ble Moth-er Ma-ry comes to me,
when the bro-ken heart-ed peo-ple liv-ing in the world a-gree,
when then night is cloud-y there is still a light that shines on me,

speak-ing words of wis-dom, let it be._____ And
there will be an an-swer, let it be._____ For
shine un-til to-mor-row, let it be._____ I

speak-ing words of wis-dom, let it be._____ And
there will be an an-swer, let it be._____ For
shine un-til to-mor-row, let it be._____ I

speak-ing words of wis-dom, let it be._____ And
there will be an an-swer, let it be._____ For
shine un-til to-mor-row, let it be._____ I

in my hour of dark - ness she is stand - ing right in front of me,
tho' they may be part - ed there is still a chance that they will see,
wake up to the sound of mu - sic, Moth - er Ma - ry comes to me

in my hour of dark - ness she is stand - ing right in front of me,
tho' they may be part - ed there is still a chance that they will see,
wake up to the sound of mu - sic, Moth - er Ma - ry comes to me

in my hour of dark - ness she is stand - ing right in front of me,
tho' they may be part - ed there is still a chance that they will see,
wake up to the sound of mu - sic, Moth - er Ma - ry comes to me

speak - ing words of wis - dom, let it be._____ Let it
there will be an ans - wer, let it be._____ Let it
speak - ing words of wisd - dom, let it be._____ Let it

speak - ing words of wis - dom, let it be._____ Let it
there will be an ans - wer, let it be._____ Let it
speak - ing words of wisd - dom, let it be._____ Let it

speak - ing words of wis - dom, let it be._____ Let it
there will be an ans - wer, let it be._____ Let it
speak - ing words of wisd - dom, let it be._____ Let it

be, let it be,____ let it be,____ let it be,____

be, let it be, let it be,____ let it be,____

be, let it be, let it be,____ let it be,____

whis-per words of wis-dom, let it be,___ let it be. And be,___ let it be.

whis-per words of wis-dom, let it be, let it be. And be,___ let it be.

whis-per words of wis-dom, let it be, let it be. And be,___ let it be.

1, 2. *3.*

mp

O Happy Day

TRADITIONAL SPIRITUAL

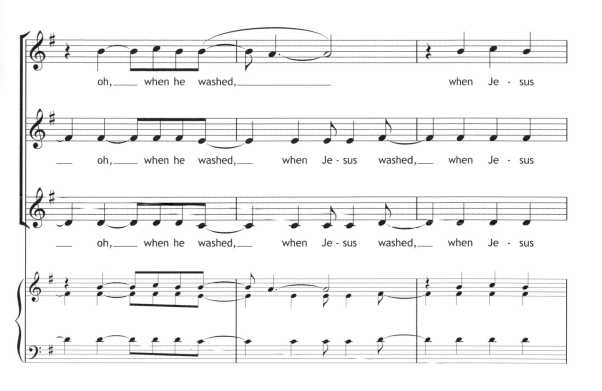

O hap-py day, hap-py day. O hap-py day, He taught me

O hap-py, O hap-py day. He taught me

Oh hap-py, O hap-py day. He taught me

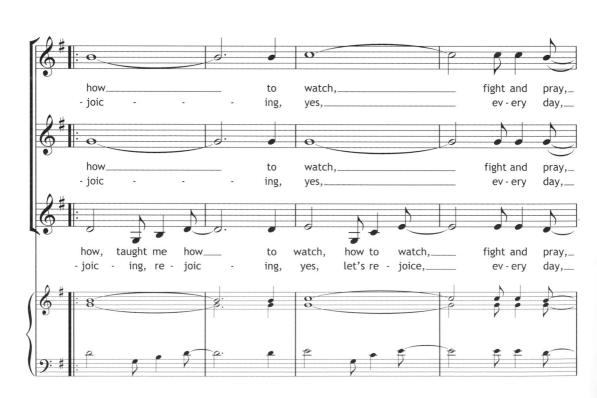

how to watch, fight and pray,
- joic - - - ing, yes, ev - ery day,

how to watch, fight and pray,
- joic - - - ing, yes, ev - ery day,

how, taught me how to watch, how to watch, fight and pray,
- joic - ing, re - joic - ing, yes, let's re - joice, ev - ery day,

Redemption Song

Words & Music by Bob Marley

from the bot-tom-less___ pit. But my hand___ was made___

from the bot-tom-less___ pit. But my hand___ was made___

from the bot-tom-less___ pit. But my hand___ was made___

___strong by the hand of the Al-might - y. We for -

___strong, made___ strong___ by the hand of the Al-might - y. We for -

___strong, made strong___ by the hand of the Al-might - y. We for -

- ward in this gen-er-a - tion___ tri-um - phant - ly.

- ward in this gen-er-a - tion___ tri - um - phant - ly.

- ward in this gen-er-a - tion___ tri - um - phant - ly. Won't you

Won't you help to sing___ these__ songs of free - dom? 'Cause

Won't you help to sing___ these__ songs of free - dom? 'Cause

help. help to sing,___ help to sing___ these__ songs of free - dom? 'Cause

Soon And Very Soon

WORDS & MUSIC BY ANDRAE CROUCH

Soon and ve - ry soon__ we are go - ing to see the king.__ Hal - le -
No more cry - ing there, we are go - ing to see the king.__

Soon and ve - ry soon__ we are go - ing to see the king.__ Hal - le -
No more cry - ing there, we are go - ing to see the king.__

Soon and ve - ry soon__ we are go - ing to see the king.__ Hal - le -
No more cry - ing there, we are go - ing to see the king.__

- lu - jah. Hal - le - lu - jah, we're go - ing to see the king.__

- lu - jah. Hal - le - lu - jah, we're go - ing to see the king.__

- lu - jah. Hal - le - lu - jah, we're go - ing to see the king.__

Fine

Should there be a - ny riv - ers we must cross, should_ there

Should there be a - ny riv - ers we must cross, should_ there

Should there be a - ny riv - ers we must cross, should_ there

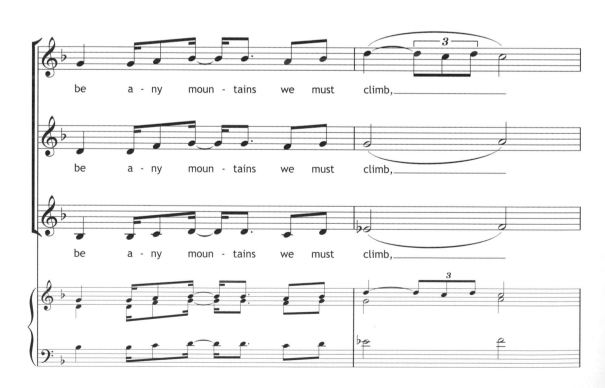

be a - ny moun - tains we must climb,_____

be a - ny moun - tains we must climb,_____

be a - ny moun - tains we must climb,_____

God will sup-ply all the___ strength that we need, give us

God will sup-ply all the strength that we need, give us

God will sup-ply all the strength that we need, give us

D.C. (verse 1) al Fine

grace till we reach___ the oth - er side.___

grace till we reach___ the oth - er side.

grace till we reach___ the oth - er side.___

Standing In The Need Of Prayer

Traditional Spiritual

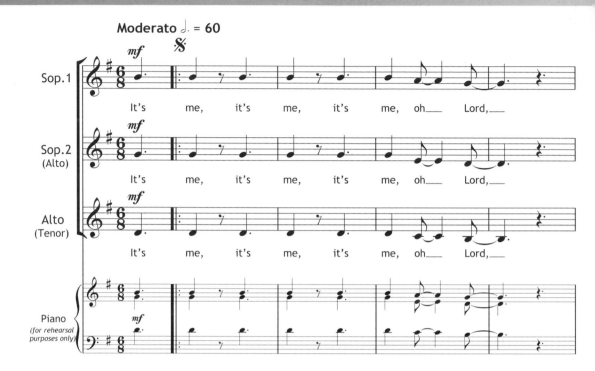

me, it's me, it's me, oh___ Lord.___ Stand-ing in the

me, it's me, it's me, oh___ Lord.___ Stand-ing in the

me, it's me, it's me, oh___ Lord.___ I'm stand-ing in the

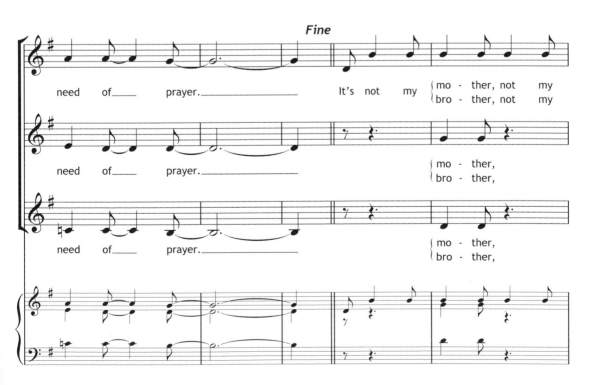

Fine

need of___ prayer._____ It's not my { mo - ther, not my
                                          { bro - ther, not my

need of___ prayer._____ { mo - ther,
                              { bro - ther,

need of___ prayer._____ { mo - ther,
                              { bro - ther,

31

fa - ther,⎫ but it's me, oh___ Lord,___ stand - ing in the
sis - ter,⎭

fa - ther,⎫ me, oh___ Lord,___ stand - ing in the
sis - ter,⎭

fa - ther,⎫ me, oh___ Lord,___ stand - ing in the
sis - ter,⎭

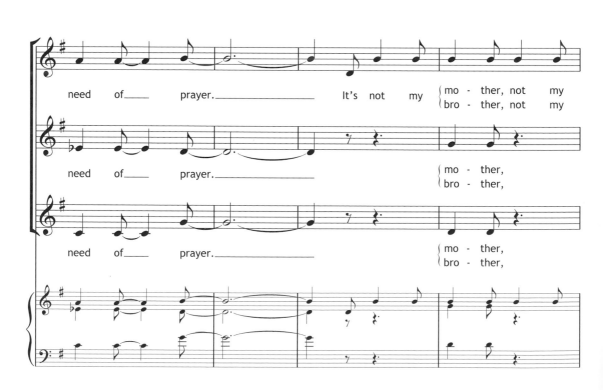

need of___ prayer._____ It's not my ⎧mo - ther, not my
⎩bro - ther, not my

need of___ prayer._____ ⎧mo - ther,
⎩bro - ther,

need of___ prayer._____ ⎧mo - ther,
⎩bro - ther,

father, / sister, } but it's me, oh___ Lord,___ stand - ing in the

father, / sister, } me, oh___ Lord,___ stand - ing in the

father, / sister, } me, oh___ Lord,___ I'm stand - ing in the

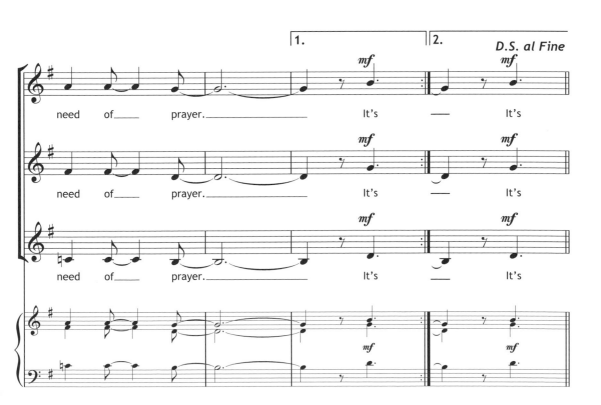

D.S. al Fine

need of___ prayer._____ It's ___ It's

need of___ prayer._____ It's ___ It's

need of___ prayer._____ It's ___ It's

33

Swing Low, Sweet Chariot

Traditional Spiritual

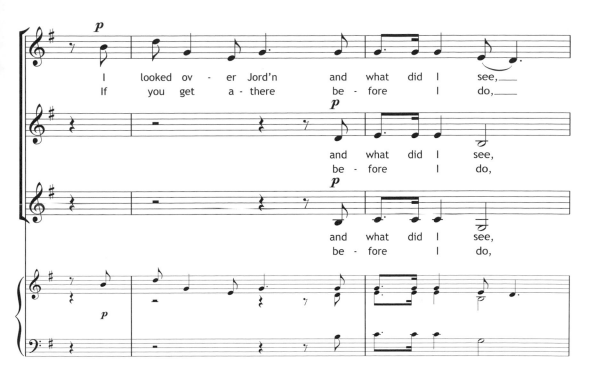

coming af - ter me,___ com- ing for to car - ry me home.
com - ing too,___ com- ing for to car - ry me

coming af - ter me, com- ing for to car - ry me home.___
com - ing too, com- ing for to car - ry me

coming af - ter me, car - ry me home.___
com - ing too, car - ry me

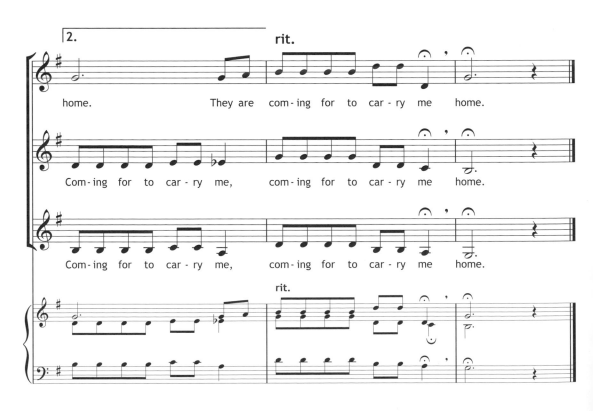

home. They are com- ing for to car - ry me home.

Com- ing for to car - ry me, com- ing for to car - ry me home.

Com- ing for to car - ry me, com- ing for to car - ry me home.

rit.

Wade In The Water

TRADITIONAL

Published by
Novello Publishing Limited
14-15 Berners Street, London, W1T 3LJ, UK.

Exclusive distributors:
Music Sales Limited
Distribution Centre, Newmarket Road,
Bury St Edmunds, Suffolk, IP33 3YB, UK.

Music Sales Pty Limited
120 Rothschild Avenue, Rosebery,
NSW 2018, Australia.

Order No. NOV016225
ISBN 13: 978-1-84609-929-8
ISBN 10: 1-84609-929-3
This book © Copyright 2007 Novello & Company Limited.

Edited by Rachel Payne.
Music processed by Paul Ewers Music Design.

Printed in the EU.

www.musicsales.com

Your Guarantee of Quality:
As publishers, we strive to produce every book
to the highest commercial standards.

The book has been carefully designed to
minimise awkward page turns and to make
playing from it a real pleasure.
Particular care has been given to specifying
acid-free, neutral-sized paper made from pulps
which have not been elemental chlorine bleached.

This pulp is from farmed sustainable forests
and was produced with special regard for
the environment.

Throughout, the printing and binding have
been planned to ensure a sturdy, attractive
publication which should give years of enjoyment.

If your copy fails to meet our high standards,
please inform us and we will gladly replace it.